# What Do You See?

Buster Books

# Created by
# Andrew Pinder

### Edited by Philippa Wingate
### Cover Design by John Bigwood

This edition first published in 2016 by Buster Books,
an imprint of Michael O'Mara Books Limited,
9 Lion Yard, Tremadoc Road, London SW4 7NQ.

The material in this book previously appeared in *Splat! What's That!*

W www.busterbooks.co.uk    f Buster Children's Books    🐦 @BusterBooks

A CIP catalogue record for this book is available from the British Library.

ISBN: 978-1-78055-459-4

2 4 6 8 10 9 7 5 3 1

This book was printed in July 2016 by Leo Paper Products Ltd,
Heshan Astros Printing Limited, uantan Temple Industrial Zone,
Gulao Town, Heshan City, Guangdong Province, China.

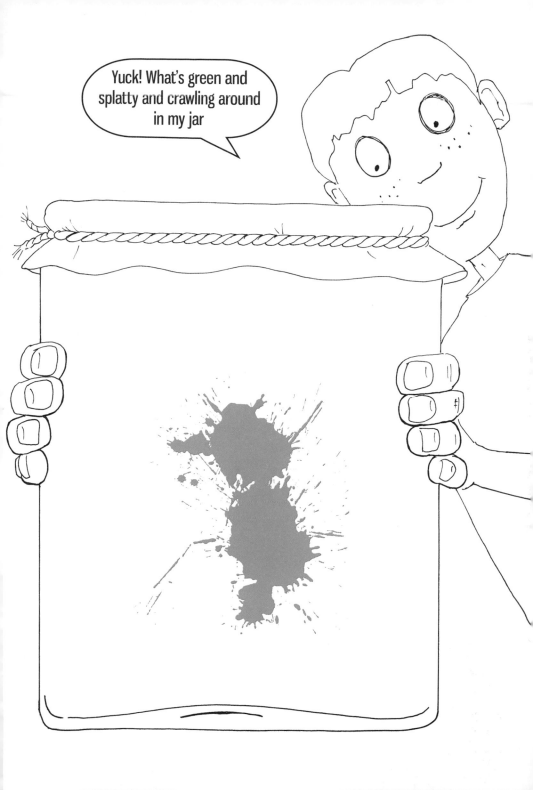

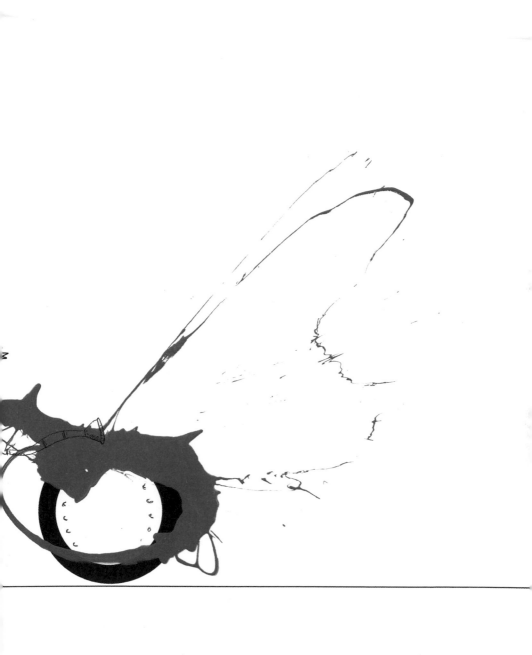

Turn the frilly ferns into dinosaur bones.

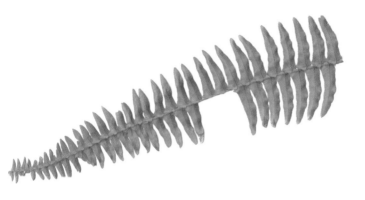

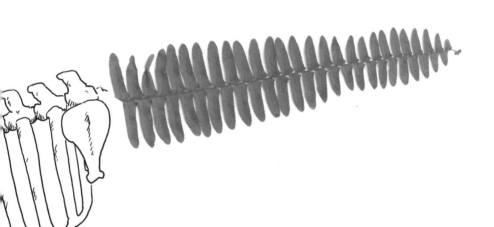

Give us silly faces and even sillier names.

Draw fairies under the pretty petal hats.

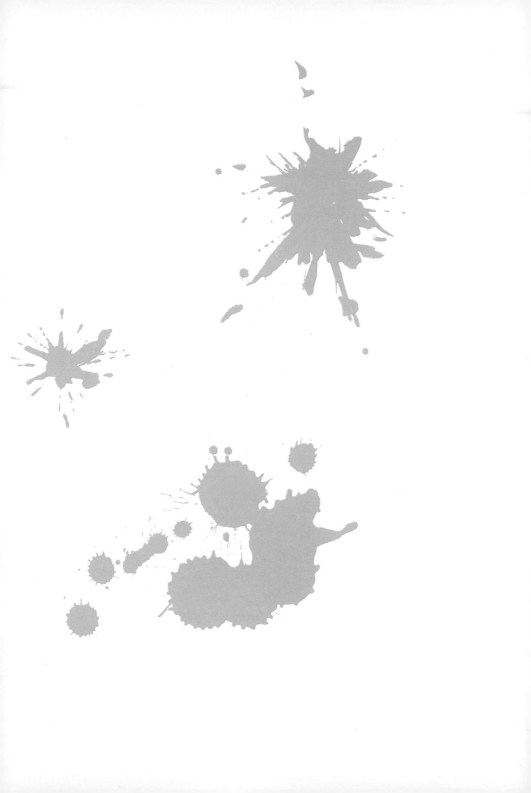

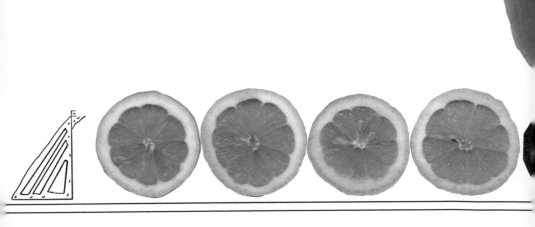

All aboard!
Turn the fruit and vegetable
slices into a chugging train.

 Draw bodies for the painted thumbprint butterflies.

Can you give us
thumbprint wings?

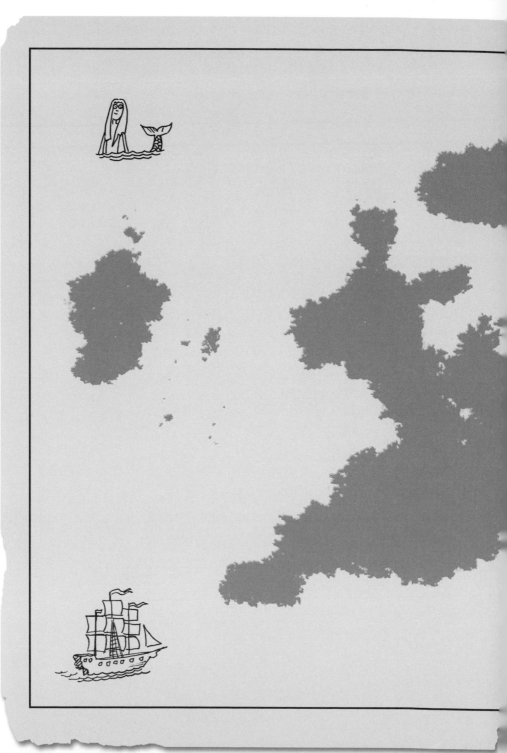

Turn the drips into hairy beasts, like me.

I am a brainy alien from the planet cabbage. Draw me a friend.

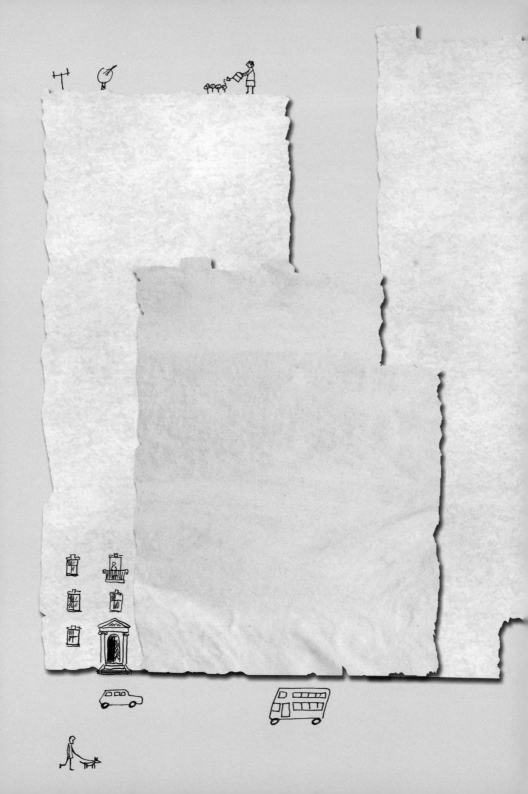

Make our paper city a buzzing, busy place to be.

What is hiding
in the herb garden?

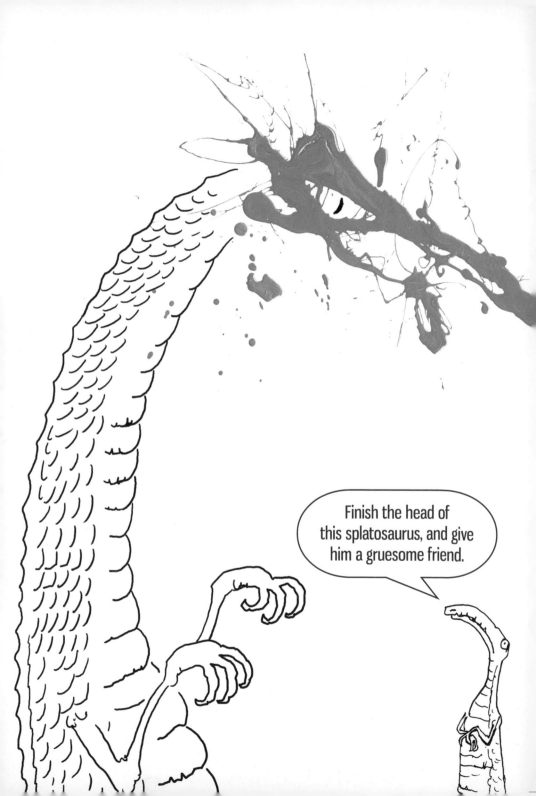

Action! What's on the old rolls of film?

Make the leaves into beautiful birds, like me.

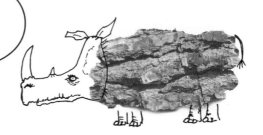

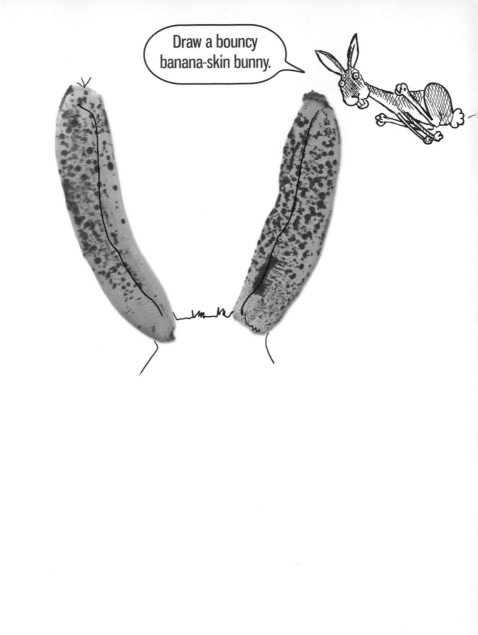

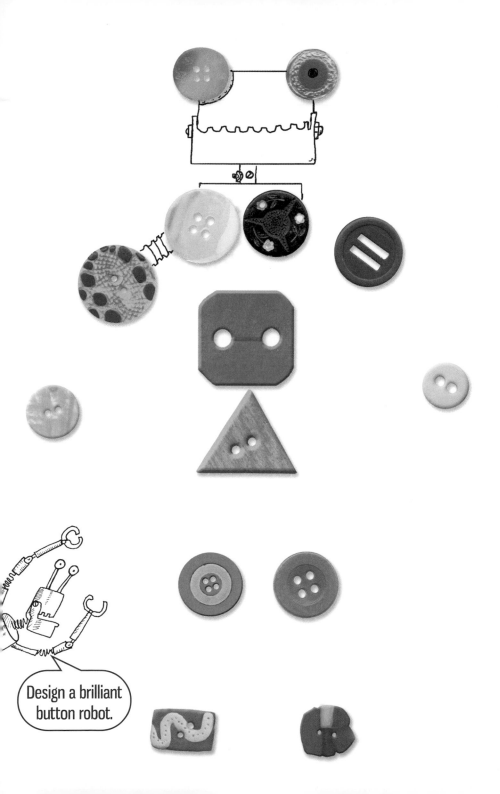

Design a brilliant button robot.

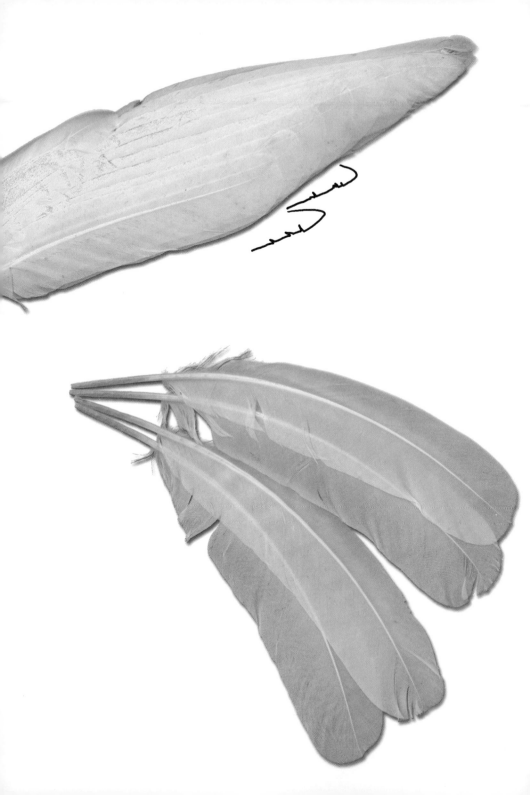

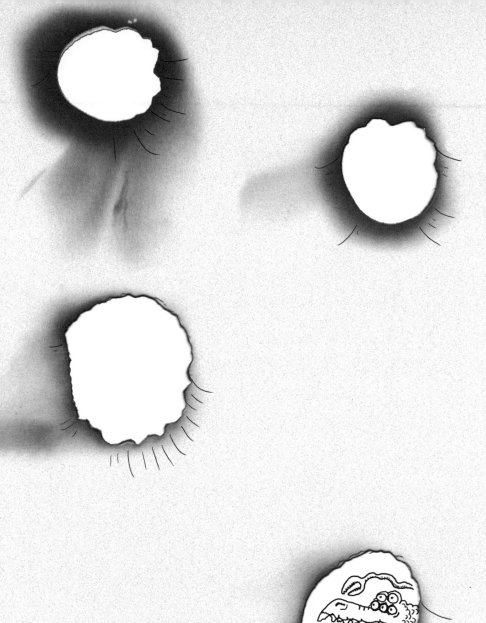

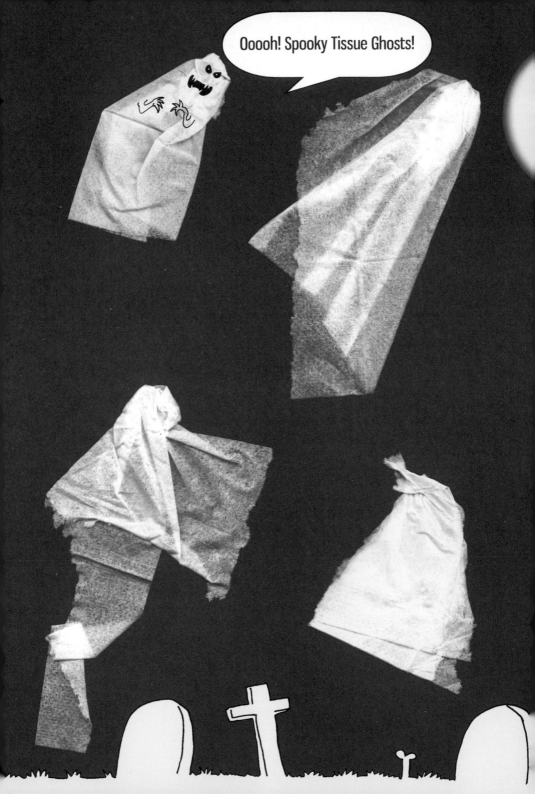

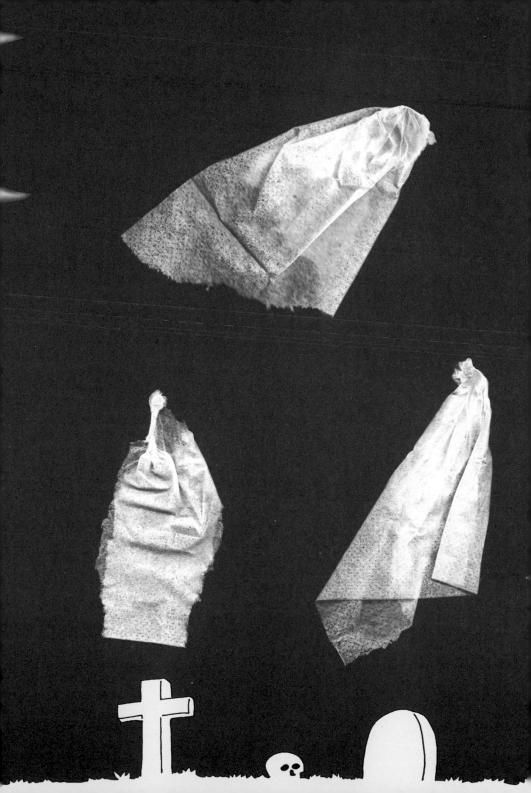

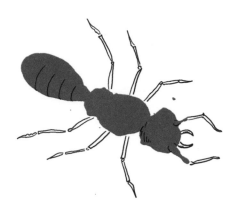

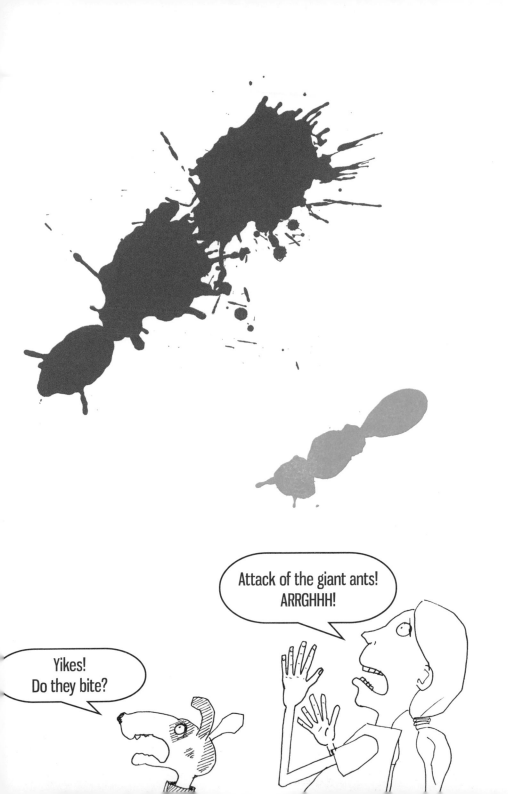

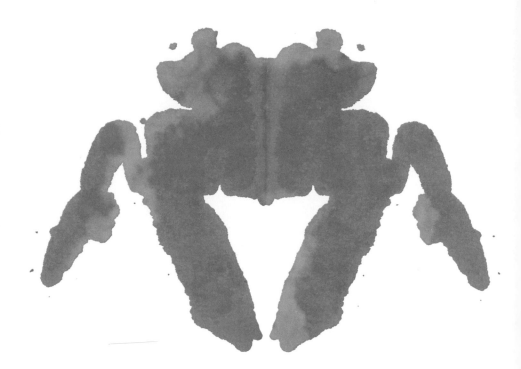

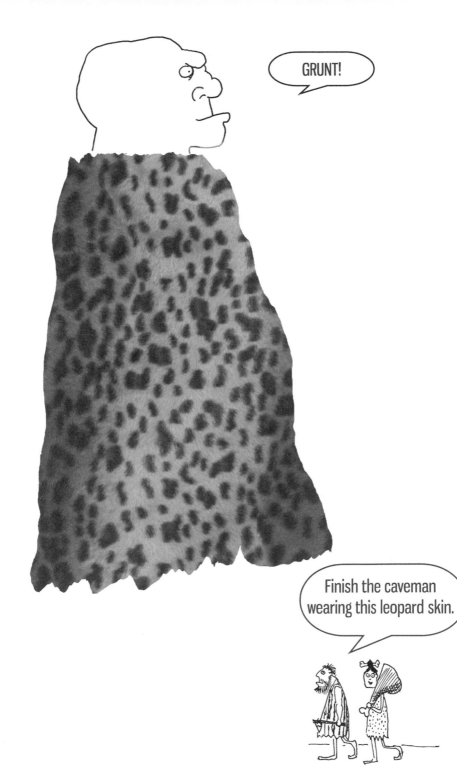

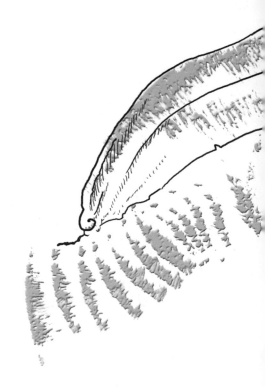

Make this paint pattern into a fearsome, fire-breathing dragon.

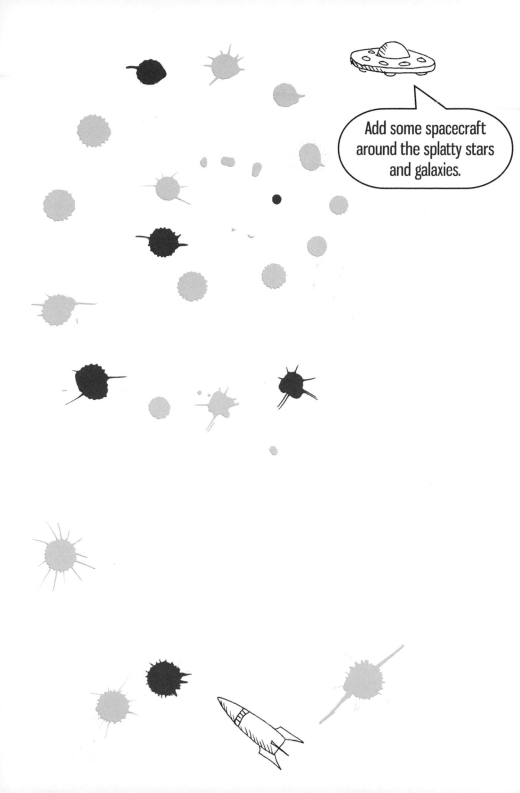

Add some spacecraft around the splatty stars and galaxies.

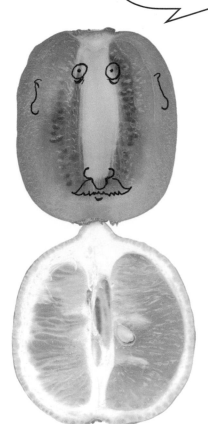
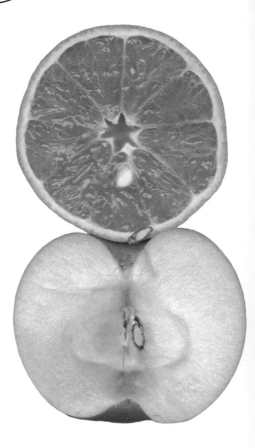

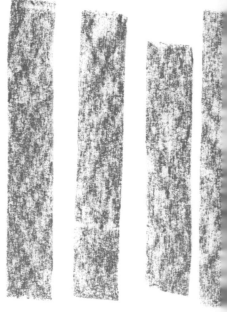

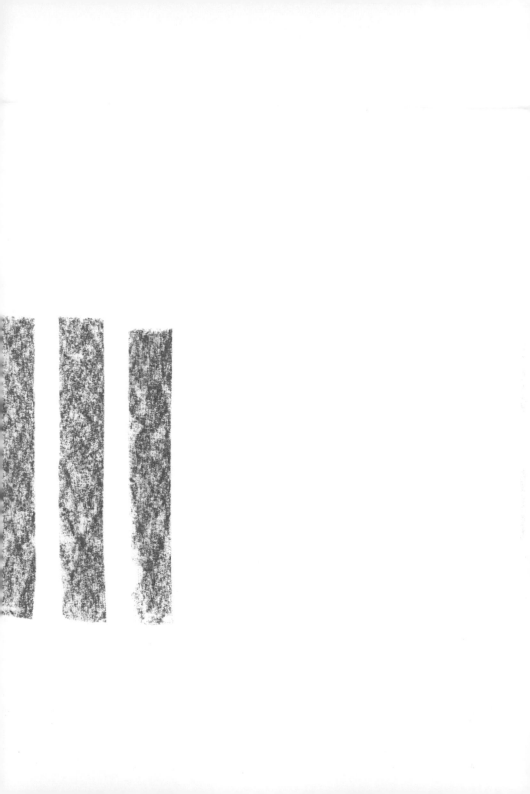

What's flying around the paper clouds?

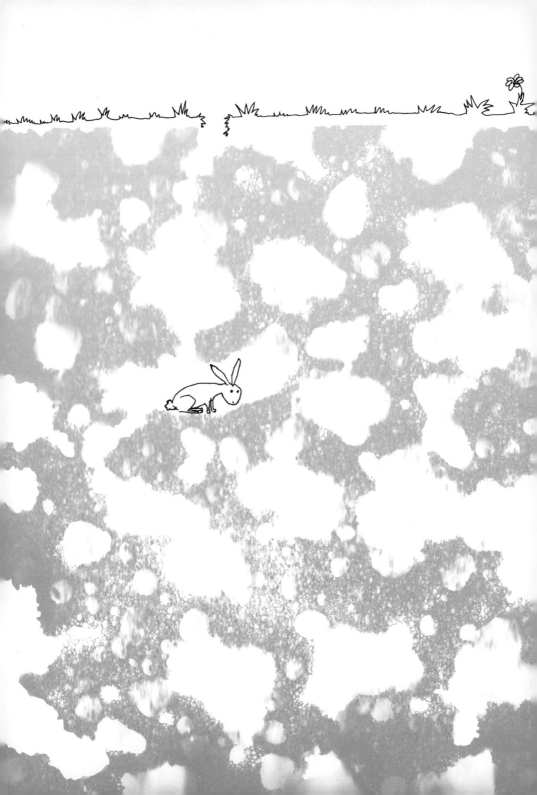

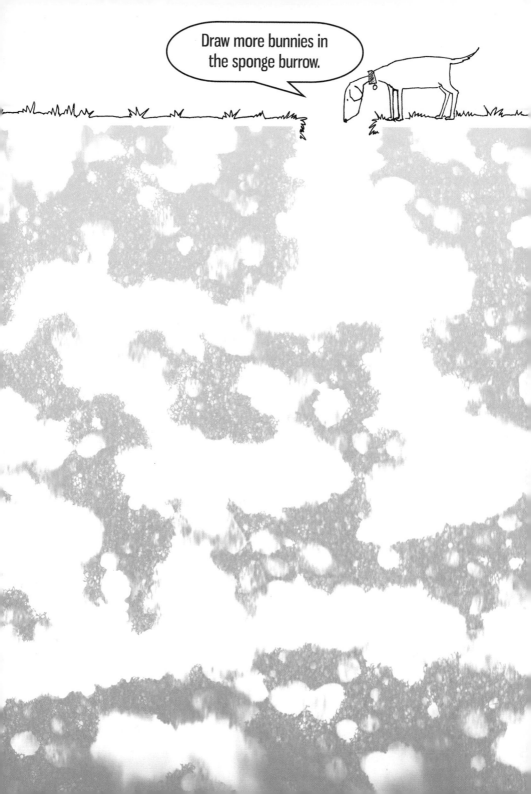

Finish the furious, flying, monster mosquito!

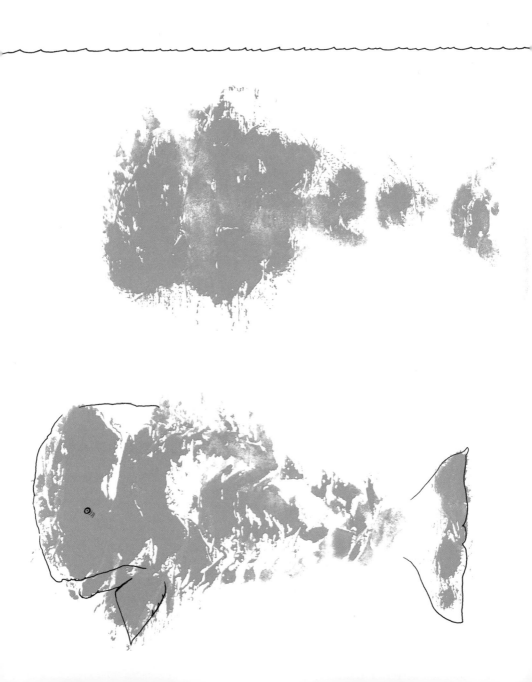

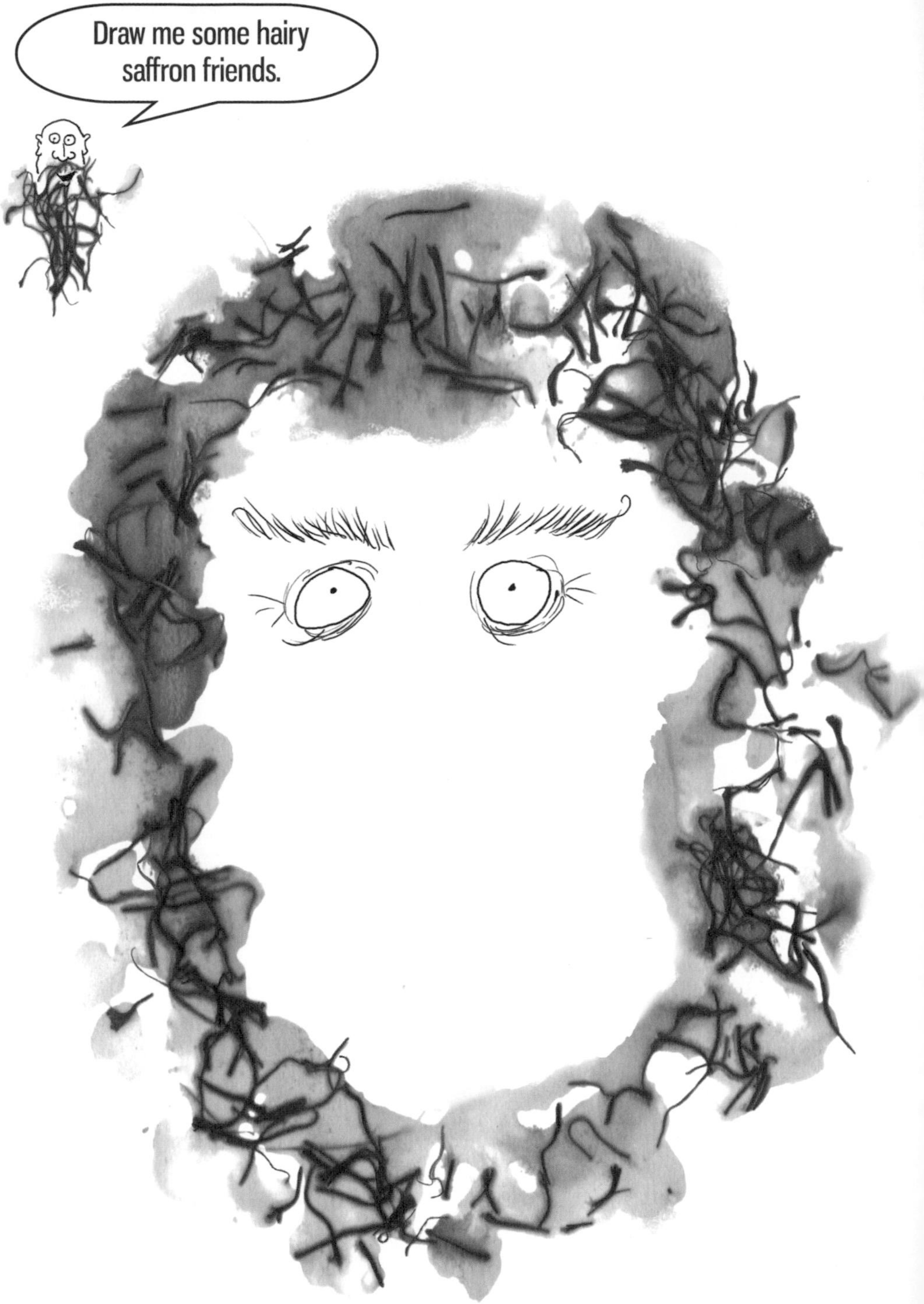
Draw me some hairy saffron friends.

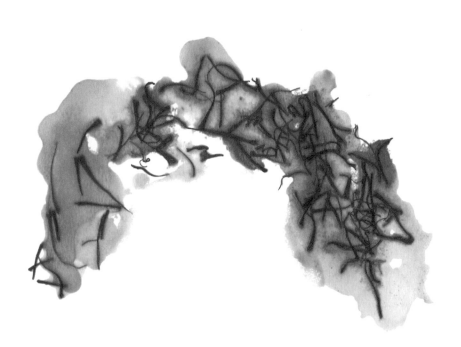

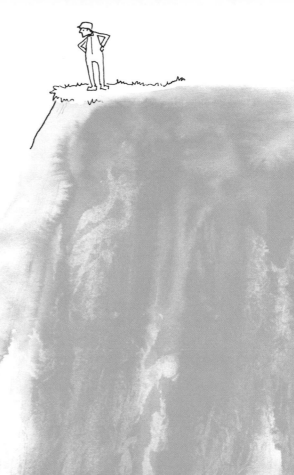

Turn this string into a night owl.

Draw more people in olive-leaf hats, ready to dance at the carnival.

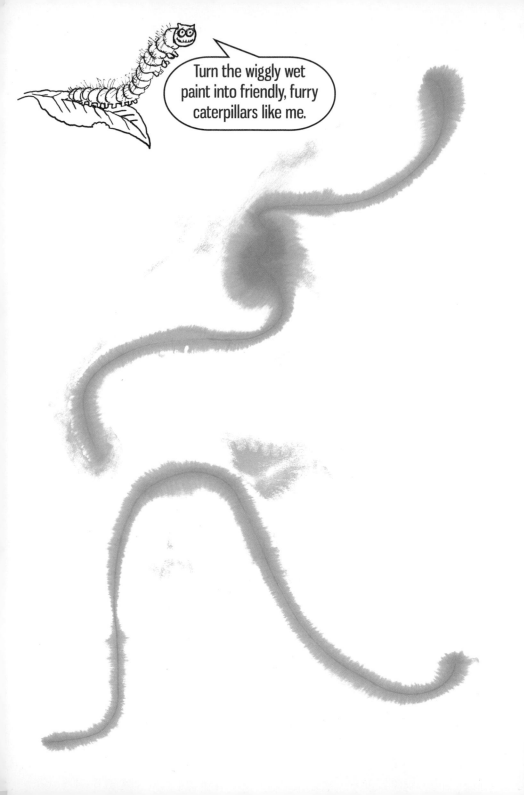